LEARN, TOIL AND WORSHIP

A JOURNEY THROUGH LIFE IN NORTHAMPTON

Northampton Heritage Hunters

LEARN, TOIL AND WORSHIP

A journey through life in Northampton

ISBN 978-0-9521997-6-2

First Published August 2011 by

Northampton Heritage Hunters

Printed in Great Britain by

LEARN, TOIL AND WORSHIP

A JOURNEY THROUGH LIFE
IN NORTHAMPTON

INTRODUCTION

Learn, Toil and Worship-A journey through life in Northampton

is produced by the Northampton Heritage Hunters history group.

Northampton Heritage Hunters was formed in 2006 and its members are all amateur, but enthusiastic, history seekers. At some time in our lives we have all been to school, worked for our living and most of us will have attended church, if only for a wedding or a funeral.

With our memories and our research into buildings and a way of life that has changed for ever we hope to encourage you to record your life for future generations.

By remembering and learning from the past we can look towards a better future.

"Capturing Northampton's past for the future"

Northampton Heritage Hunters

CONTENTS

Worship

Contributors

Christopher Glazebrook

Derek Hawkins

J.M. Clements

Jack Plowman

June Wilkes

Linda Kemp

Marion Chapman

Mary Judd

P. Potter

Reg Spittles

Rita Z. Wills

Rosalyn Willis

Val Knowles

LEARN

The first 8 Chapters deal with
"Happiest Days of your Life" ??

Chapter 1

ST GEORGE'S WITHOUT THE DRAGONS

At the start of the 20th Century Northampton was about to expand far more than people realised. If you walked from Regent Square along Barrack Road, past Royal Terrace, you came across first the Holy Sepulchre School, and then nothing until the Barracks. Eight years later the area between those two buildings became the site for the new St George's School. From there, walking on towards Kingsthorpe Hollow, you would have passed the market garden area that sloped down to the river, known as Semilong.

The School Gates, Barrack Road 2011

The site for the school was bought for £2900 and the contract for the buildings was £13,185, a princely sum in those days. Opened on September 1st 1908, on a site covering just over an acre, St George's stood on an elongated plot of land that stretched from Barrack Road through to St George's Street, and was gated at both ends. It consisted of two buildings, the Infant and Junior school was a square structure situated at the St George's Street end and the Senior school was an oblong at the Barrack Road end. An Edwardian design of red brick, with high windows to allow plenty of light, it had a very warm and stately appearance. A cutting from the paper two years later in March 1910 reported that having been a garden area before, horseradish was forcing its way through the asphalt playground and needed to be eradicated. It wasn't going to give up easily was it?

I lived in close proximity so I was enrolled in the infants in 1939. In those days St George's Street was still partially residential and boasted the George and Dragon pub, and on a Saturday night the strains of the piano could be heard from quite a way away. Marlow's shoe factory stood on the corner of St Patrick's Street, Payne's furniture shop a little further up, the Chinese Laundry at the top and Mrs Starmer's outdoor beer house at the bottom. All these were on the right-hand side, opposite the school.

Harding Terrace had its share of shops too. Mrs Felton kept a sweet shop on the corner of Upper Harding Street, and the cat always slept in the window in a box of sweets. There was a fish and chip shop, Mrs Crouch the grocer, Scott's whose shoe shop had a double window, and the aptly named Mrs Bedford the greengrocer. There was also a newsagent. So as opposed to today, it was a busy and very vibrant neighbourhood.

I don't remember a great deal about the first year in the infants, Miss Allen took the first class, but I do recall Miss Barton in the second year telling a bible story from memory each morning while she watered her plants. The hall was central with surrounding classrooms and even though it was wartime they always managed to put a Christmas tree in the hall, which seemed enormous to us.

Miss Baker the headmistress wasn't easily forgotten. She was as round as she was high and always wore floor length dresses in brown. Moving very fast across the hall, appearing like a chiffon cloud that was propelled by some means other than walking. She was feared by some, but was always nice to me.

Progressing through Miss Cordy's class, the final junior class was Miss Griffin, who prepared pupils for the Eleven Plus exams. This would decide whether it was to be high school or not. Much to my surprise I passed and chose the high school in St George's Avenue, but I was elected to go to the Notre Dame. Usually a private school, it would accept a few scholarship pupils. After a few months though, with my father in the army and so many things we still had to provide, my mother struggled financially to keep my brother and I, and payments for the things I needed at Notre dame. It was decided I had to leave. So one Monday at 9.00 am I was taken to St George's Intermediate School to see Miss Redfearn the headmistress. Standing there in my new gymslip, white blouse, red tie etc, I felt very apprehensive, but after a chat everything seemed a lot different, and I had no trouble settling in. I had some catching-up to do and new friends to make, which came very easily.

My new teachers were Miss Stratford, art, Miss Fisk for English and history; Miss Lawrence, French; Miss Blick, maths; Miss Nichols, geography and needlework (and later French too); Miss Allen, sports; Miss Abbot, music; and Miss Sharman, cookery.

Each pupil was allocated a house and in our school they were named after the four national saints. The system of credit, discredit, or detention meant you could have points for or against you. At the end of the month they were all totalled and read out at Assembly. It made you aware that your actions affected other people too.

There weren't many lessons I disliked apart from art and cookery. My efforts in art were viewed by Miss Stratford with disappointment in the first year, the second year with irritability, and thereafter with jaw-clenched frustration; so no credits there. Cookery I just found boring. The Centre was on the opposite side of the road near to Regent Square so we walked in the usual crocodile with what ingredients we could muster because of rationing, to face yet more cheese straw delights. I did get in trouble once through my friend Carol, who hated the lesson too. We were arranged in lines of tables and Carol (who had an impish sense of humour) was two rows away. She decided to throw a wet dishcloth at me, which missed so I picked it off the floor, and without looking first, returned it with a throw Ian Botham would have been proud of. To my horror Miss Sharman had walked along the row and, yes, bull's eye! It sat squarely on the back of her head, so no credit there either. The future Mayoress too!

I liked English and history best. I learned a love of books and reading from Miss Fisk, joined the library at eleven and remain a member still. Music came to the fore more when we were rehearsing for Speech Days, which were held at the Guildhall.

I think it was in the second year that my friend Marion was given the duty of ringing the hand bell to signal the change of lesson. She was the only one in the class who owned a wristwatch so there weren't any other takers. Now Marion was small, the bell rather large and she had to run from the top corridor through the hall and down the lower corridor then back to class. It seemed that after the first swing the bell was spurred-on by its own momentum with Marion hanging on for dear life. She arrived in class breathless but always on time.

Sports were played on the Racecourse and were interrupted severely in 1947, which has been well-documented regarding how long the snow lasted. During those days we had the games lesson in the assembly hall. Normally we played our inter-house hockey matches, rounders etc. and races on The Racecourse.

Maths was OK, except I would get a decent mark for Algebra then lose marks for Geometry because once again I can't draw.

Miss Nichols was always a very popular teacher. She had such an even and gentle style and gained our interest from the start of the lesson. Miss Lawrence, who originally took us for French, left and we were all so pleased when Miss Nichols took over. Miss Lawrence was a good teacher but very, very stern.

After a while Miss Redfearn's place was taken by Miss Taylor as the new Head. A lot younger, she brought some new ideas. Miss Allen asked permission to run a table tennis group after school and permission granted, we proceeded to dismantle the stage and two parts of it were soon turned into the tables. Miss Taylor had an interest in drama and started a similar after-school group, which was great. I enjoyed it. Mostly I did backstage work where I was happiest. She decided one time though, that we were to do a piece from Jane Eyre with me as Mr Brocklehurst, to be performed as an end of term treat. I didn't feel comfortable on stage and during rehearsal it obviously showed because she kept telling me to look haughty. For the first time costumes were to be hired. Oh, excitement indeed! When they came though, to put it kindly the aroma was quite strong. At dress rehearsal she seemed quite pleased with my performance; I probably looked haughty now, because my nose was in the air keeping it as far away from the costume as possible. Nevertheless, the play was well received at the end of term and Miss Taylor highly delighted.

There was always a great emphasis placed on self-discipline which worked because if you did anything wrong you felt very silly and childish. Like most girls of that age though, we were prone to fits of the giggles and one class really tested our self-control. The teacher was rather small and had to really stretch to reach the top of the blackboard. As she stretched, about half an inch of knee-length elasticated pink bloomer was exposed. It was a case of eyes front, stare straight ahead and risk grinning. I especially daren't catch Carol's eye.

Oh yes, we did country dancing too, but the problem there was very few of us were the same height. You would either be paired with someone too small, or in my case someone far too tall. Prancing about to *The Dashing White Sargeant* didn't always look as graceful as it should have done.

About thirteen of us started a little club of our own after school. I can't remember whose relation it was, but someone had a disused bake house attached to their house. We got permission to use it and as it was my friend Carol's idea, and the number of members, we called it "Carol's Baker's Dozen Club". It lasted quite a while too.

1949 came and it was time to leave and go to work. Before we went our different ways, we were allowed a leaving party, which was fitting because we were the last Intermediate class. The school system was altered, and eventually St George's became a middle school, then in 2005 approaching its centenary, it was demolished to make way for the new Castle Primary.

THE TIME CAPSULE BURIED HERE MAY BE OPENED IN 2033. WE CELEBRATED THE OPENING OF CASTLE PRIMARY SCHOOL ON 23RD APRIL 2007 WITH 356 PUPILS ON ROLL.

Sadly there are only two reminders of the original school, one in St George's Street on the wall in stone lettering stating "St George's Council School", the other near the main gate on Barrack Road in a circular plaque depicting St George slaying the dragon.

I've given a brief insight into my time at St George's and you may say it's a pity I couldn't have stayed at Notre Dame, but I don't regret one day I spent at St George's. I remember the staff with respect and have often used things they taught me in later life.

I've been as accurate as I can, but have realized lately, that Father Time has a habit of taking your memories and either hitting the scramble button, or keeps them to himself! Sneaky isn't he?

Rita Z Wills 2009

Chapter 2

A CONTRAST IN EDUCATION

In 1950 my parents along with many other ex-service men and families, became the first tenants on the 'award winning' Kings Heath estate. Our immediate neighbour was 'a cockle shell hero' of World War 2 and most shared a common bond and all had served their country well.

I soon made new friends and along with them attended Spencer infants School, later moving to the newly opened Gladstone School. Now Earl Spencer School.

Our first day was spent in awe of this beautiful modern building, with it's bright interior, highly polished floors, and Venetian blinds, demonstrated by our teacher, to open on a dull day and close when the sun shone on our books.

This I recall was a good school with excellent teachers. Pupils were given equal opportunities to do well. The boy who sat next to me later became headmaster of Cherry Orchard, now closed along with many others.

I do not remember any discipline problems although Spencer estate had many large families, discipline started at home and teachers were respected.

For me this soon changed again, as our parish priest Fr.Galvin advised my mother of her duty to send me to a Catholic School, and I was duly transferred to Saint Mary's R.C. on the Lower Mounts. This drab Victorian building was a far cry from Gladstone School.

I nevertheless enjoyed the religious education which set me in good stead for life. The Nuns intrigued me with their long black habit and pious ways. Although they could be very strict in all aspects especially obedience, and good manners.

The head mistress at the time was Sister Marie Julie. Sister Austin was the very elderly headmistress of the infants. Father

St. Mary's School and a view of the Mounts

Galvin was a frequent visitor and the children loved him.

The children came from many different backgrounds, some of Irish decent, also non Catholics, and poverty was very evident.

The girls from Nazareth House along the Barrack road attended, and were easily recognized as they wore a navy and white uniform and each had the same bobbed hair.

The classes were very large, the desk's set in two's and in columns, then tiered upwards. One class I recall a column was set aside for girls with head lice! I was so aware of this discrimination and knew then that it was very wrong. The toilets were disgusting, no flush, only a wooden seat and bucket upon which one would hover if desperate!

There was no canteen at first but children could get a hot meal at the Regent Square Chapel this was like a 'workhouse' and very frightening for a small girl. The big boys from Campbell Sq School went there, and I could not possibly enter! So I went to my Grandmothers in Charles St.

Lessons on the other hand were very good. English was taught well, and speech, drama, and music encouraged.

St. Mary's R.C. School – the corner of The Mounts and Lady's Lane.

Christmas time we had the usual concert, a large chest full of costumes was brought into the classroom. I hoped to wear the blue velvet, and play Prince Charming, I would learn all the lines, but never got the part.

I often recall some events during that period. On the 28th January 1953 we prayed for Derek Bentley who was executed that morning, his friend Christopher Craig had fired the gun killing a policeman but was only sixteen at the time. In 1998 Bentley was given a posthumous pardon.

June the 30th 1954 there was a partial solar eclipse we children gathered in the grounds overlooking the Notre Dame. Thrilled to escape lessons and watch the spectacle.

I have many other good memories of those days and have valued the lessons taught there for the rest of my life.

The school was completely closed in the 70s and later Demolished. The job centre stands now where the school once was.

Rosalyn Willis. 2011

Chapter 3

ORANGE, BROWN, GREEN AND BLUE COAT SCHOOLS IN NORTHAMPTON.

Orange Coat School.

Northampton's Orange Coat school was founded in 1710 on an endowment by John Dryden of Chesterton and further endowed in 1734 by Zachariah Herbert. The school was situated in Abington Street at the corner of Wood Street (now the Abington Street entrance to the Grovener centre). The purpose was to *'clothe, educate, and apprentice twenty boys of the town of Northampton'*. The uniform, as laid down in the will of John Dryden, *'a blue coat faced with orange colour with brass buttons, a knit cap and stockings of orange colour'*. By 1819 it seems that the orange colour had disappeared as the Trustees made a ruling that the uniform be returned to the original colours as the school was sometimes referred to as the Blue Coat school. More of this school later.

Brown Coat School.

Northampton's Brown Coat School was endowed in 1753 with donations from James, Earl of Northampton of £1,200 and several other gentlemen of the county. The then Corporation bought with the donations an estate in Bugbrooke. One third of the income from the estate was to *'clothe, and educate a number of boys belonging to the poor freemen of the town'*. Two thirds *'to annually clothe twenty poor men of the town and presenting them with ten shillings' (50p today)*. This school was situated at the bottom of Bridge Street. The uniform as the name of the school suggests was brown and of a style of that period.

Green Coat School

Northampton's Green Coat School was endowed in 1761 by Gabriel Newton of Leicester, who bequeathed most of his property for the purpose of educating poor children in Leicester, Ashby-de-la-

Zouch, Earl Shilton, Northampton, St. Neots, Huntingdon, Buckingham and Hertford. The purpose of these schools was *'clothing, schooling and educating twenty five boys of indigent and necessitous parents of the established church of England. Each boy to be allowed annually or once in eighteen months, a green cloth coat, waistcoat and breeches, not under 20d per yard, one shirt of flaxon cloth, not under 13d per yard, with stockings, cap etc, and the residue yearly paid to teach the boys reading, writing and arithmetic and the singing of psalms and the toning responses in divine services in the parish church. No boy to be admitted if parents receive relief from the parish; nor any town to be entitled when the creed of St. Athanasius is not publicly read in the service of the church'.* All this required more than the £26 per annum provided by the Newton bequest, and the corporation made good the annual deficit of about £60.

The will of Mr. Newton was contested by his heirs and for a time the payment of £26 was suspended pending the court case. The corporation bore the extra expense for some time but the Green Coat school, who shared the premises with the Brown Coat school, closed for several years but was reinstated and restored to being part of the Bridge Street school some time before 1799.

The Brown and Green Coat schools continued at Bridge Street until it was demolished and a new school was built with a masters house attached. The boys still wore their Brown and green coats. The Green uniform disappeared about 1818 and soon after the Orange Coat school reverted to their original colours. In 1819, the Bridge Street school changed to a Blue uniform. Henceforth both the Brown Coat school and the Green Coat school were dressed the same and referred collectively as the Blue Coat School.

In the middle of the 19th century extra places were available in Bridge Street and the Orange Coat school moved from Abington Street. They both retained their distinctive uniform and the School was known as the Blue Coat and Orange Coat School until it closed in 1921. In 1898 the uniforms and boots were still made to measure.

The masters house and school as it is today 2011

The new school building and masters house in Bridge Street was erected by the Corporation in 1811 as denoted on the plaque on the front of the building. It seems almost certain that the building was designed by a gentleman by the name of Luke Kershaw who was Mayor of Northampton in 1807. He played a prominent part in the town affairs. He was landlord of the Goat Inn in Gold Street, then of the Peacock Hotel in the Market Square. He advertised in the local newspapers that he was "an architect, surveyor and auctioneer". He died in 1821.

The building cost £1,670 and built of brick at the front and stone at the rear. This followed the trend of this period to replace stone with brick for new buildings in Northampton. Either side of the plaque are two alcoves to house two statues from the original building, one dressed in brown, the other dressed in green both of a style of the 18th century.

The Blue Coat boys were mainly selected from the tradesmens' sons, while the Orange Coat boys were still genuine "poor boys". Blue Coat boys wore (preaching) bands and long trousers. The Orange Coat boys wore white stiff collars and black tie and breeches with brass buttons. Unlike today where a school uniform is supposed to be a great leveller, the uniforms at the Bridge Street school very much kept the class system alive.

From an article in the Northampton Independent Dec. 1921;

'The school, in the early days of the Dorman Swimming Shield carried all before it in the competition, has just won the Spanish Swimming Trophy given by Sir William Butlin for the best percentage of swimming and life saving certificates amongst the elementary schools of the town. They have also a swimming trophy of their own given by an Old Boy, Mr. Arthur Gadsden, who was one of the survivors of the 'Lusitania' disaster'.

From a document called;

RULES AND ORDERS OF THE BLUE COAT SCHOOL
NORTHAMPTON
SETTLED BY THE TRUSTEES OF THE CHURCH CHARITIES ON
APRIL 26 1847

No boy could enter the school unless they lived in the borough, were under 10, were able to read fluently, were acquainted with the catechism, and knew the rules of arithmetic. They had to remain there until 13, and were required to be regular and punctual in their attendance and tidy in their person and apparel (suspension if they were not).

That in addition to the sound secular education the boys be religiously instructed in accordance with the principle of the United Church of England and Ireland as now established, that they attend divine worship in the parish church of All Saints every Sunday morning, afternoon, and evening and at such other times the Trustees

appoint, and they meet half an hour before the times of the services and proceed to the church under the superintendence of the Master.
School Hours are;
(From March 1st to October 31st)
6-30 to 8am, 9am to noon, and 2am until 5pm and for the rest of the year an hour shorter in the afternoons. Holidays shall be fourteen days at Midsummer, fourteen days at Christmas, two days at Easter, and every Saturday, and public examination at such time the Trustees appoint'.

Chronicle & Echo June 1981 –Susanne Dilley.— The Statues

In 1981 the Statues were reinstated to the front of the Blue Coat and Orange Coat School. They have been restored to their original colour of Green and Brown dating back from the two original schools.

The !8th century statues

29

Remarkably one of the visitors to the exhibition of the newly restored statues was a Mr Joseph York, aged 93, who attended the school in 1898.

The statues have been in safe keeping for the last few years in All Saints Church and later in the Central Museum. The figures were repaired by sculptor Noel Black and repainted by Northampton artist Eileen Nicholson for her major project in her final year at Lincoln College of Art.

The original 1811 building still stands at the bottom of Bridge Street complete with the statues, one green and one brown, but is now a restaurant. Even if the use of the building has changed over the years, since the school closed in 1921, it is still standing unlike a lot of our beautiful buildings and our town's history.

The inspiration for writing about these particular schools is that my grandfather, Charles Montague Leach, attended The Blue Coat and Orange Coat School at the beginning of the 20thcentury.

My grandfather 1904 - 2nd row kneeling, 3rd from the right. He wore the Orange Coat School uniform.

Val Knowles 2011

Chapter 4

A TALE OF TWO ERAS.

"Can you remember the name of your Headmaster?"

He thought for only a second then replied, " Fatty Saunders", Mr F P Saunders he corrected. I was talking to my father-in-law Bill Tuckey about his days at Kettering Road School.

During our various conversations I had realised that Bill and I had attended the same school, but with a 30 year gap.

The history of the school is very interesting and mirrors the social changes that were occurring throughout England during the Victorian times. These changes were brought in with the introduction of the Education Act of 1870.

The Elementary Education Act of 1870, was introduced on 17th February 1870 by the Liberal M.P. the Hon. William Forster, (commonly known as Forster's Education Act,) and set the framework for the schooling of all children between the ages 5 and 12 in England and Wales. The Act was not universally accepted because it was felt in some quarters that mass education would make the labouring classes, with their increase in knowledge, dissatisfied with their lives and liable to revolt. The churches, which were funded by the State with public money to provide education for the poor, did not want to lose their influence on the young.

Britain's industrialists, on the other hand, feared that their status in world trade was being hindered by a lack of an efficient education system.

The Act established the foundation of English elementary education. Gladstone's Liberal government became increasingly involved and finally, in 1880, made attendance compulsory for children until 12 years old.

A Board of Education could be petitioned to investigate education provisions in their area. This was done by comparing the results of a census of existing school places with the number of children of school age recorded in the census. If there were a substantial shortfall, a School Board would be formed. Board members were elected by a vote, and were paid either from the Poor Rate or the Municipal rate.

In Northampton the Board governing these schools (called Board Schools) was formed on January 13th 1871 and consisted of 11 members, with offices at 4 St. Giles Street.

Kettering Road School was one of the first Board Schools to be built (the first schools in fact were Vernon Terrace and Spring Lane), with a temporary school being opened on 26th November 1877 in Queens Road. It had 3 board members. The Headmaster was Mr. John Williams, with Miss Platt as assistant, there were 76 children admitted.

Kettering Road School

The construction of the new Board School on the Kettering Road/ Clare Street junction, was begun in 1877 with the formal laying of the foundation stone being carried out on Monday 23rd of April 1877. The inscription on the stone read; "This foundation stone was laid by William Adkins, Esq. J. P., Chairman of the Board, April 23rd 1877, Bland and Cossins, Architects. Edward Barlow, Builder".

Beneath the stone was placed a bottle containing copies of the Times, the Mercury, and the Herald newspapers, with a number of copper and silver coins struck during the present year. In addition was a newspaper with the article covering the ceremony and identifying those who attended. The school was eventually opened on Monday 14th October 1878, with a final cost of £12,200 (the estimated cost being £7,984), with a capacity for 467 boys, 360 girls and 500 infants.

Mr. Simpson M. Fraser was the Master, Miss Elizabeth Sharwood Mistress, and Mrs. Annie Covington Infant's Mistress.

Each child admitted needed a birth certificate and a schoolbook, and was expected to sit an introduction examination. This exam threw up an interesting fact, that many of the children from Private Schools were "very backward".

Any child who had a 100% record for attendance in a full year was given an award. This came in the form of an Attendance Medal. To win this award the child was allowed only one half day sickness and one half day to attend a Sunday school outing.

The medals were of white metal, on one side they bore the inscription "Reward of merit" with the borders of laurel wreath, on the reverse side "delay not - time flies", over a winged hour – glass: and beneath the legend "Awarded for attendance".

A Bronze medal was awarded for five years full attendance, again with the exception of one half days sickness and one half days allowance to attend Sunday school outings!

Northampton already had a range of private boarding and day schools, for the not so poor, such as Thomas Crass school in St. Giles

Street in 1762.

New charity schools had also been established to supplement the Free Grammar School founded by the grocer Thomas Chipsey in 1541: the Orange school in 1710 supported by endowments from John Dryden and Zachariah Herbert.

The Blue Coat school established in 1753 with a gift of £1000 from James Earl of Northampton: and the Beckett and Sargeant school for girls, which opened in 1735.

Between them the charity schools catered for around 100 children.

I first saw John Clare Secondary Modern School in September 1955.

In my life 1955 was a milestone year; my family had moved house from Far Cotton, were I was born, to a brand new house (with a bathroom) at Eastfield.

Although I was destined for a brand new school, Cherry Orchard Secondary Modern School was unfinished in time therefore I attended 'Ketts' for one year.

In those days schools were split into three sections; namely Infant's, Junior's and Senior's.

I was also being transferred from Junior's to Senior's, which meant that at 11years old I would be mixing with 15year old boys, with all the testosterone that went with boys of that age.

On my first morning when the register was called there were two absentees. The addresses of the boys sounded familiar to me so after school I walked around the estate and discovered where they lived. The boys became my best friends throughout school and beyond.

"Pop" Wright was the Headmaster at the time and although I had little dealings with him I think he was near to retirement. His assistant was Mr Wilson.

Whereas Mr Wright seemed reserved for the Head of such a tough school, Mr Wilson fitted the school perfectly. He was a figure of authority with a reputation for discipline, which was enhanced by the fact that he administered the punishment (mainly in the form of the cane).

Strangely enough he also took the sports lessons.

I remember him marching us up to the Racecourse for football and rugby, us boys already changed in our games kit, him his only concession being his trousers tucked in his socks, whilst wearing big, old fashioned brown boots.

Bill also remembered his games period, again on the racecourse with Mr. E Kirkham.

Good sportsmen were encouraged and given time off lessons to practise, Bill excelled at rugby and high jumping and said that he enjoyed the privileges that came with success. He also remembered that the main punishments were either the cane or staying behind after school. He spoke of the poverty that many of the children lived in, torn clothes and worn out shoes, these memories still seemed vivid even today.

We also discussed swimming. I remember walking to the Mounts Baths for our swimming lesson and seem to remember a terrifying lady named Mrs. Howard who taught us. I was one of the lucky ones who could already swim the more unfortunate ones who couldn't were attached to a harness, which was connected to a rope held by Mrs. Howard. She would brace herself then pull with all her strength dragging the poor boy through the water. Most of those who experienced this torture found it very difficult to ever enter the water again.

Bill encountered similar swimming experiences only at Barry Road school baths.

He also remembered Mr. S. B." Fuzzy" Harris, but could not remember the subject that he taught.

Other memories of 'Ketts' (the correct name of the school was John Clare Secondary School, but everyone including Bill called it 'Ketts' or 'Ketts College of Knowledge'), included alighting the bus at the Picturedrome, near a cake shop, and buying a bag of "stale cream cakes" all of which we consumed before we reached school.

Another memory I share with Bill is that of using the rear entrance to the school on Spencer Road. This was done mostly if you were late or to watch the blacksmith, which made you late. We share the thrill of seeing the sparks flying and the anvil ringing as the craftsman of Matthews Ltd. produced tools and implements for customers.

I left 'Ketts' in 1956 moving to the brand new Cherry Orchard Secondary Modern School on Birchfield road. There I joined as a second year pupil and was one of a full complement of three classes. There was also a third year, but this consisted of just one class so we supplied the majority of members of the football, rugby and cricket teams, needless to say in those early years we were beaten in most games by bigger, stronger older boys.

I think my education from both schools suffered due to the after affect of the eleven plus and the feeling of being a failure, plus the upheaval of moving home and loosing all my old friends. It was at Nene College where I discovered a real pleasure in learning, along with an ambition to achieve better things for myself.

Bill on the other hand seemed to really enjoy his time at Ketts and had the opportunity to go to the Grammar School on a Scholarship at fourteen he did not take up this offer as he felt it would put too much financial pressure on his parents.

One final point regarding this attractive red brick Victorian School when it was opened it catered for boys and girls, in fact on the main Kettering Road entrance above the left hand door it reads 'Boys'. Above the right hand door it is blank, although it looks as if the stone has been altered. This mystery was cleared up when I found out that on the 29th August 1921 the building formerly used as a school for boys and girls, was reopened as an Intermediate school for boys only (the major alterations being carried out during the summer break).

'Bill' in his school uniform

"Old boys dinner 'Fuzzy' Harris centre"

I would like to dedicate this work to the late "Bill" Tuckey who sadly passed away on December 11th 2010, twelve days short of his 95th birthday.

"Bill" really enjoyed his wonderful life, and filled other peoples lives with his good humour.

Derek Hawkins 2011

Chapter 5

BOUGHTON SCHOOL

My mother, Mrs Gertrude Rench, worked as a teacher at Boughton School from 1927 to 1948.

Mrs. Gertrude Rench 1937

She took the children from six to eleven. There was an Infant Teacher, but my mother was in charge. She was unusual in that she married and had a daughter, me. She taught everything, from Games to Maths. If a child was naughty she could cane him or her on the hand. Every year she got one or two pupils through the Eleven Plus. The Inspector, who called frequently, was pleased with what he saw.

While she was there, a new school was built. The old coal fire had gone and there was central heating. In front of the school was a playground where she taught the children exercises; at the back a big field with slides and swings. The cottage where we lived was about five minutes' walk away. We went for country walks in which my mother told us things about the birds and flowers. She kept us busy all day long.

My father was a blacksmith; he had a workshop at Sywell. He dealt with cars as well as factory machinery. He could repair anything and frequently did.

I was at my mother's school for eight years, finally gaining a Scholarship to the High School. My mother had a Teachers Certificate but was far better educated than this meagre qualification suggests. I am proud to be her daughter.

Mary Judd   2010

Chapter 6

MY SCHOOL – KINGSTHORPE GROVE: 1923 to 1932

I started at an Infant entrance in St David's Road, with my friend Dennis Kempshed, having progressed from there across the hall, as we used to say, to the Boys' Junior and Senior Sections.

My teachers for the 1st and 2nd years' Juniors' were Mr Hill and Mr Chambers.

Having eventually become a Senior I list the teachers by name for their individual subjects;-

Woodwork: Mr Bliss. Science: Mr Amos.
History: Mr Foyle. Geography: Mr Tilley
Art (Drawing): Mr Barnes. Arithmetic: Mr Swain.

When I first entered the Junior and Senior Sections the Headmaster was Mr Leach with Mr Piggot as an Assistant Headmaster but it wasn't long before Mr Leach retired and took charge of the boys' summer camp at Grendon and Mr Piggot then became our full-time Headmaster.

In those days our classes could be as large as 48-50 boys and at one time we had 2 so-called temporary classrooms added in the playground. I paid a visit a few years ago and I noticed the temporary classrooms were still there. Also the old Girls' Cookery School had now become a Senior Girls' Section?

One thing I was disappointed about was that in the hall the raised platform had been taken away to make more room, but also in my time at the school in the hall on one wall in very bold gold figures were the names and the years of when boys had passed for the Grammar School as a credit to the school and also were the names of students who had been killed in WWI, these had all been removed. I was very saddened to think that pride had been forgotten!!!

To pursue various sports we always used Kingsthorpe Recreation Ground as we had no facility for sport in the school area, one side of the area was St David's Road and the other side was allotments and open fields so any balls that went over the walls were lost balls, also in those days there was a long wall right up the centre of the playground separating the boys from the girls' and infants' section, at the top of the playground were 2 classrooms – one for woodwork and one for science, the woodwork room was in the boys' side, the science room was in the girls' side so a small door was there to make use of the science room.

In the summer for swimming we would march down to the old Kingsthorpe Mill site down Mill Lane where we had a swimming baths and children's paddling pool, in those days the swimming pool was large enough for us to qualify for our sixty yards swimming certificates, all of this was sited on the river, in the winter those that wished could go to Barry Road School because they had an indoor heated swimming pool. I never went myself because you had to walk there and back across the Racecourse (too far for me I'm afraid).

Discipline varied from teacher to teacher, they were allowed to give you 4 strokes with a cane if needed. But for anything considered to be serious would mean a visit to the Headmaster's Study where 6 strokes would be given and your name in the book against your character for end of term report, my recollection is that Mr Tilley was the worst for making use of the cane, he had lost his right arm in WWI but he was very good with his left arm!!!

Although I started at the "Grove" we used to get an influx from the Church School in Kingsthorpe Village known as "The National" because all Church Schools' pupils had to leave when they were about 9 to 10 years of age and most would come to Kingsthorpe Grove, among these were 3 of my cousins, Ron and Norman Spittles, they lived in Ruskin Road, we also had 3 brothers by the name of Hawtin – Nat, Sol and Walt – those 5 comprised the large part of our football team, another pair of brothers were the Dales' boys, I understood the older one was killed in WWII. Another boy was

"Ginger" Jacobs. I believe he was killed in Kingsthorpe in a car accident whilst on leave from the Navy, his parents had a large store on the main road.

Our Caretaker was a Mr Wallington who lived in St David's Road, his son David was also a pupil. Some pupils came on a short-term principal for various reasons. Colonel Harding from the Barracks on the Barrack Road sent his 2 boys for as long as he was stationed in the town, we also used to have business people's sons who came for extra teaching to make sure they passed for the Grammar School on the Billing Road, it was cheaper than paying to enter, this extra teaching was known as Cramming", one of my own cousin's who went to St Paul's School in Semilong Road told me himself that because the Headmaster there realised or thought he had a pupil who was a bit brighter than average gave him extra attention and in consequence he did pass and went to the Grammar School, which was a credit to the school, he left at 16 years' of age which made it awkward to get a job in the Boot Factory because he was 16 with no experience for a boy of that age.

A few names I remember were – Lew Malle, Sid Cox, Frank Morris, Harry Judd, Stan Roberts, Bertie Basford, Woolley, Clarke, Howe, Bob Berrill, Dawes, Jess Ley, Harry Brown – plus the ones I have already mentioned in my ramblings?

Reg Spittles   2006

Kingsthorpe Grove School—Established 1906

Chapter 7

KINGSTHORPE GROVE SCHOOL/ THORNTON'S PARK

When I was 12 years old I started at Kingsthorpe Grove Secondary Modern School and as the school only had a small area for sports and the main hall for PE, we went to other sites for sports including Bective Boys' School to use their gym, Kingsthorpe Recreation Ground for hockey and the Racecourse for tennis. For all other sports including rounders we used Thornton's Park.

One game of rounders sticks in my memory, as I was waiting in line to take my turn with the bat the girl in front of me decided to take a couple of steps back to hit the ball and knocked me out. The next thing I remembered after that was a sea of faces looking down at me and I had to sit out the rest of the game.

My Mum and her friends had other memories of Thornton's Park and they used to talk about how in the 20s and 30s before the Thornton family gave the Hall and grounds to the town, once a year they opened the grounds to the public and put on a Fete and games. As most working class families could not afford holidays and days out, this day was looked forward to with growing anticipation by both parents and children as a chance to have fun and meet friends.

Linda Kemp   2011

THE SCHOOL BOARD MAN

Many people will remember Mr Hawtin the "School Board Man" who checked-up on the truants and their families. He did the work for at least 20 years and probably longer as I remember him from my school days in the 1940s and 50s and I have neighbours in their 40s who remember him visiting their parents.

He was one of my neighbours in Ruskin Road and he was at school at Kingsthorpe Grove with my Mum. Living so close to him put us local children off "playing the wag" as he was always around on his bike and seemed to have eyes in the back of his head and the ability to be in two places at once. He only came to my house once, when I was twelve and had been very ill and had been off school for two months. I was so bored I would sit and look out of the window for hours and he saw me and came to ask my Mum why I was not at school as I had never been away from school before.

I have a friend who was always playing truant, whose older brother and his friends would write notes to take to school, supposedly from her Mum or Dad, excusing her from school. Then she would spend the day playing at Kingsthorpe Mill and the Dallington area. The school became suspicious and sent Mr Hawtin to her house and she was found out and told if she did not start going to school she would have to stay for another year.

I don't know what he would think of the truanting nowadays and the children you see in the town and the shops when they should be at school. Although nowadays with the size of the town you would need many more "Mr Hawtins".

Linda Kemp   2011

Chapter 8

CASTLE HALL SCHOOL

Castle Hall School was established around 1870. The first Principle was Mrs. Thorpe. By 1895 the Principle was Mrs. T Bogle, the daughter of Mrs. Thorpe. The school afforded excellent facilities for High Class Education to young ladies under the direction of Mrs. Bogle, and her predecessor, whose thoroughly practical qualifications in each branch of tuition had secured the warmest commendation of a wide circle of clients in all parts of the country.

The handsome building was situated on a portion of land formally occupied by the ancient castle, a historical relic still in existence at that time and in its' original position was the old postern gate by which admission to the grounds could be obtained.

Tennis courts and extensive grounds surrounded the house which accommodated upwards of 20 boarders and 30 day pupils.

Singing, French, German, Violin, Drawing, Painting, Dancing, Callisthenics and Swimming were taught. Pupils were prepared for Local University Examination.

It was widely acknowledged the school was situated in one of the healthiest parts of the town.

By the turn of the century the school had relocated to St. Matthews Parade and advertised that it was situated on the outskirts of Northampton and that country walks were easily obtainable.

The building was modern, especially adapted with well ventilated, airy bedrooms, separate cubicles for Senior Scholars and electric light. Examinations were held each term and pupils were prepared for Cambridge Local, Matriculation, Froebel and Music Examinations.

Instruction included Religious Knowledge, English, History, Geography, Mathematics, Science, French, German, Theory of Music, Needlework, Drawing, Drilling and Class Singing.

Castle Hall School, St. Matthew's Parade

A large play ground and tennis courts were to the rear of the building and on the adjacent Recreation Ground (the Racecourse) Hockey and Netball were played.

In the 1920's Castle Hall School moved for the final time to Abington Avenue Congregational Church rooms. In 1928 Miss Olive Vasery was the principle. Castle Hall School, now a primary school for both boys and girls, stayed at Abington Avenue until 1944 when the school was closed.

The school motto was:-
'NOT FOR SCHOOL, BUT FOR
LIFE WE LEARN.'

A footnote:-
The grand daughter of Mrs. Bogle was Joan Hickson, the definitive "Miss. Marple" of Agatha Christie fame.

Val Knowles 2011

TOIL

After schooldays for most of us the next stage in our lives was work.

The next 8 Chapters relate to work and the workplace.

Chapter 9

CANALS

Before the advent of the canals many roads were impassable in bad weather and it took up to 10 horses to pull a wagon loaded with two tons of freight. Inland towns were at a disadvantage as most coal and heavy goods were carried down the coast in colliers and other small craft so coastal towns and cities and towns with navigable and wide rivers were growing while towns such as Northampton were static.

With the introduction of the canal system the price of coal was halved as one boat towed by a horse could carry fifty tons or more in weight. When coal, slate or building materials were unloaded corn or other goods could be sent back to the industrial towns in the North. Boots were sent from Northampton for export and it is said that Napoleon's Grand Army marched to Moscow in 1812 wearing Northampton made boots. There had been little economic growth in Northampton even after the Nene had been made navigable in 1761 except for mills and timber and coal yards at regular intervals along the river.

Roper and Coles map of 1807 still shows that a great area of Northampton running down to the river was orchards and gardens with little or no housing or manufacturing.

The opening of the canal arm from Blisworth to Northampton in 1815 was a success and the town's prosperity increased greatly with the advantage of cheaper fuel and most mills changed from water to coal power.

The average person's life was also changed for the better as building materials such as slate and brick were delivered in large numbers for newer housing, cheaper foodstuffs also became available – better cooking utensils and Staffordshire crockery replaced old iron cook pots and wooden bowls.

The main hauliers in the East Midlands and Northampton area were Pickfords who had a wharf at Blisworth and Fellowes, Morton and Clayton who operated out of Braunston and the canal basin at Market Harborough. (They were still in existence until 1948 when they were taken over by British Waterways.)

Although the economy of the canals suffered with the introduction of the railways in 1845, most agricultural products such as timber, hay, corn, malt and straw were still carried by water, as they could be loaded anywhere on the canal side without having to use expensive railway sidings. The canals, of course, depended on a workforce to operate them. The first boats were worked by two people, usually a man and a boy, and the power of one horse. They did not have a sleeping area on the boats but slept ashore. It is known that some of these men were the Navvies who had helped to build the canals. The families of the men lived ashore in rented cottages with only a few wives accompanying their husbands on board. With the competition from the railways in the 1840s the carrier cut the men's rate of pay and they economised by moving their families aboard the boats to use as crew, thus saving the cost of housing ashore. Work was hard for both men and women as on certain parts of the canal system such as changing from one canal to another the horse could not be used for power and the boats had to be manhandled by everyone on board.

The wives also had to contend with washing and drying clothes, raising the children, cooking in a confined space and helping to maintain the boat and equipment.

The interior of the small living area would be kept immaculate with all the brass on the cooker being kept highly polished. All wall space would be covered in decorative Staffordshire plates and every shelf covered in crochet worked by the women and girls. The floor would be covered in newspapers to keep the dust of coal and grain off the surface.

Water cans and all utensils, which were usually made by a local tinsmith, would be highly decorated, also many of the boats themselves were decorated. The highest style of decoration was the Braunston style consisting not just of the normal roses and flower decorations but also paintings of castles and scenery.

All of the domestic needs of the families could be met at the canal side villages which as well as a water supply usually had a small general store, pub, chandlers, blacksmiths and stabling.

The boat people also developed their own style of clothing including intricate bonnets for the women. Some carriers even supplied the men with a uniform.

Entertainment, weddings, christenings etc would usually be held in the canal side pubs. Boatmen's Institutes were also set up where meetings etc could be held.

Since the Education Acts of the late 1800s children had been attending local schools at the "turn around time" but this was only for a few days a month.

In 1944 the Secondary Education Act was passed which required 200 days a year school attendance which could not be met by the "turn around time" and many families began to move back ashore into cottages. The canals were still busy right up to the mid-20th century and coal, steel, timber and foodstuffs were being carried. The last delivery of grain by canal/river to Whitworth Mill in Wellingborough was in 1969. Although trade still continues on the canals, a great deal of the traffic is now recreational and the days of the traditional boat family is a thing of the past.

Linda Kemp 2010

Northampton Lock

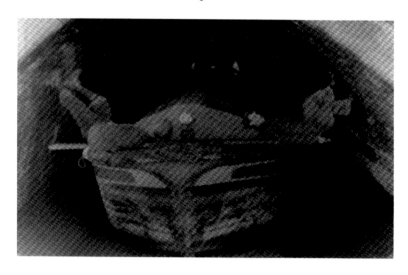

By 1827 registered 'leggers' were employed. They would wait in a hut close to the entrance to the tunnel. Then 'leg the boats through the tunnel'.

Chapter 10

THE NORTHAMPTON BOOK TRADE

Eighteenth century booksellers sold a wide range of products including patent medicines, paper hangings, musical instruments, lottery tickets and artists' materials.

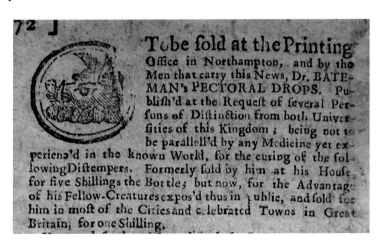

William Dicey and Robert Raikes actively promoted Dr Bateman's Pectoral Drops in the Northampton Mercury, bottles could be purchased "At the Printing Office in Northampton, and the men that carry the news". The drops, "famed for the Colic, Pains in the Limbs and Joints, Ague, and all ailments of the Breast and Bowels", were available to surgeons and shopkeepers on "good allowance" from John Cluer, a well known London printer. In addition, Cluer's Printing Office at Maidenhead in Bow Churchyard, near Cheapside, was the warehouse for "Daffy's Elixir", another label associated with Dicey. A treatise published in 1726 names John Cluer, William Dicey and Robert Raikes, as "the persons concerned with" Benjamin Okell, inventor of Dr Bateman's pectoral drops.

John Cluer was married to Elizabeth Dicey. Their son, Dicey Cluer, baptised at St Mary Staining 1 March 1703, died young. The parish register of St Mary le Bow records his burial on 6 November 1713. When Cluer died in 1723 his share in the pectoral drops passed to Elizabeth. The following year she married Thomas Cobb, her late husband's foreman, at St Anne and St Agnes, Aldergate, 31 May 1729.

The Northampton Mercury for 15 June 1730 shows William Dicey formed a new partnership with Benjamin Okell, Thomas Cobb, and Robert Raikes to continue the production and distribution of the drops. However, in 1736, Cobb assigned the Bow Churchyard premises and London business to his brother-in-law, William Dicey, including Cluer's original share in Dr Bateman's drops. The London Printing Office and wholesale warehouse now came under the supervision of Cluer Dicey, William's eldest son and business partner. The firm flourished in Northampton and Bow Churchyard. Its main activity was the publication of the Northampton Mercury and cheap literature, especially traditional ballads and chapbooks, described as "small histories" in contemporary trade catalogues. They developed a national distribution network, and regularly sent goods to North America.

On 12 November 1753, William and Cluer Dicey entered into an agreement with Richard Marshall of Aldermary Churchyard, Bow Lane. Both printshops specialised in "Woodcut Royals", popular at the time. William died at Northampton 1756. The 1764 catalogue issued by Cluer Dicey and Richard Marshall lists over 1,000 pictorial prints, 150 small histories, and nearly 3,000 ballads. William's descendants continued to publish the Northampton Mercury until 1885.

In 1792 William Birdsall (1749-1826) acquired the business and premises of John Lacy & Son, booksellers and stationers, situated at the bottom of the Drapery (the corner now occupied by Nationwide Building Society). This establishment was certainly in the possession of Henry Woolley between 1752 and 1756 before it was purchased by John Lacy. By 1777 Lacy needed additional space and leased a tenement in Drum Lane from the Wardens of St Thomas's Hospital at an annual rent of five guineas. The name Abel, first occurs in the apprentice list for 1787. James Abel, a poor boy from Derbyshire, served his apprenticeship partly under Lacy, then continued with Birdsall "for two and a half years at £26 per annum, exclusive of board and lodging". At the conclusion of that engagement, he secured the shop of Mr R Miller in Gold Street (adjoining the Rose and Crown Inn), later moving to the Market Square.

William Birdsall was appointed Deputy Postmaster of Northampton in 1801, on the resignation of Miss Warwick. The local postal service run by Birdsall, and his son James, taken into partnership in 1823 along with his brother Robert, was very efficient. In fact, Northampton never had an official penny post. A report of 1835 to Francis Feeling states: "The arrangements made by the postmaster at Northampton are highly creditable to him. There are

89 villages in the delivery of Northampton, the whole of which (with the exception of two) are delivered daily".

By 1826 James Birdsall was the sole owner of the business, his younger brother having died at the age of 25. After James died in 1840, his widow Anne (formerly Hills) carried on alone until 1845, when she married George Norman Wetton.

Birdsall entries in the parish register of Ellerburne, Yorkshire, indicate Robert Birdsall had five children, Ann (27 Dec 1747), William (9 Oct 1749), Anthony (7 Nov 1751), Francis (9 June 1754), and Hannah (15 March 1767). Anthony Birdsall was still living at Ellerburne in 1790. His son Richard (recorded in the 1830 Poll Book of Northampton, as Bookbinder, Wood Street) was baptised there on 26 November. In 1806 Richard Birdsall was apprenticed to his uncle, to learn the bookbinding trade. It was Richard's son, the famous bookbinder Anthony Birdsall (1819-1893) that established the firm's international reputation.

Christopher Glazebrook   2010

Birdsalls' on the left in a drawing by George Clark of Scaldwell

VOL. II.   NUMB. 41.

THE Northampton Mercury.

The South PROSPECT

Kingsthorpe

MONDAY, *February* 5, 1721-2. [*To be continued Weekly.*]

NORTHAMPTON:

Printed by *R. Raikes* and *W. Dicey*. Of whom may be had Land Tax Receipts
Affeffors Warrants, Funeral Affidavits, &c. Likewife all manner of Stationary
Wares, as Shop-books, Pocket-books, Paper, Pens, Ink, Wax, &c. Likewife
Dr. *Bateman's* Pectoral Drops, and *Radcliffe's* Purging Elixir : The firft fam'd
for the Colic, Pains in the Limbs and Joints, Agues, and all Ailments of the
Breaft and Bowels. The fecond is the very beft of purging Medicines ; witnefs
the many Certificates we daily receive from our Readers and their Friends.
Thefe Medicines are fold at 12 d. the Bottle, with printed Directions how to
take them, and Certificates of their Cures.
(Price of the Mercury Three Half Pence.)

Chapter 11

A PRINTERS TALE

Clarke and Sherwell Printers were a well-known part of Northampton for many years, from before the First World War through to the early 1980s.

Their story began in 1908 when three young men met in Victoria Street, which was then situated opposite the Police Station on the Mounts. With their sights firmly set on the future, they were discussing an idea, to start up in the printing trade. They were John S Clarke, George H Sherwell and Herbert Smith. All had served apprenticeships in printing; George Sherwell and Herbert Smith were with Mr Rogers of Wood Street, and John Clarke from the 1880s with John Taylor of Gold Street. He went to London for a time before returning to Northampton to resume his work here. The first premises was a converted three-story house, which was No 14 Victoria Street. The ground floor was used as the machine room, the first floor held the office and composing room, leaving the top floor for storing space. So they began and, at that time, the many boot and shoe factories in Northampton had never used printed matter before, but when John Clarke introduced two-colour printing they took the advantage to use it for advertisements. Within two years Clarke and Sherwell had gained a reputation for the quality of their work and with the increase in demand the factory soon outgrew the first site and in 1910 had to move to 28-36 Kettering Road to enable them to add a photographic department. These premises later became Law's Timber.

By then expansion was well under way and they were producing full colour literature including catalogues not only for the home market, but for firms abroad as well.

By 1913 more space was needed, so the decision was taken to acquire some land on the Kingsthorpe Road, which was sparsely built on at that time. The piece of land was where Asda the Supermarket is today, but then Thornton Road and the estate were yet to be built. The new building was to be designed by George Sherwell and they employed Mr P Hawtin for the construction. When it was completed in 1914 it had a distinctive Tudor-style frontage plus a rose garden which was unlike any other offices in the town. For many years it remained a very classy part of the Kingsthorpe Road known by everyone. It had been mistaken for a private residence on quite a few occasions.

Ever seeking improvement they learned that a new method of printing had been introduced on the Continent. This was an innovative method which was called photogravure, whereby an engraving is produced on a metal plate by light acting on a sensitive surface. They bought presses from Germany and brought over German fitters to install them. They were the first in England. Mr G Meredith, who joined the firm in 1914, had spent two years studying the method, and later when Cecil Clarke, John's son, joined the firm in 1915 they joined forces to develop the process further with the advantage of being able to produce the highest quality of richness and brilliance.

Through the formative years the firm had not neglected the workforce, for it had encouraged a very active social club, which included photography, of course, bowls, tennis, cricket, football, drama, outings and musical evenings could be enjoyed after work. Mr Sherwell who had a house near the works had a very large garden which he made available for many of the activities. Also through the years, many times members of staff were used as models for advertising too.

In 1941 Clarke and Sherwell merged with Raphael Tuck printers and this brought an even larger production of millions of greeting cards with the added distinction of being asked to produce Royal Family Portraits, and personal Christmas cards for Winston Churchill, Clement Atlee and Field Marshal Montgomery.

Some years later in 1964, they became part of the British Printing Corporation and it was then the old picturesque office frontage was demolished to make way for a completely new building 1960s style, because with more modern methods the development of four-colour printing allowed them to turn to producing mail order catalogues.

More changes were yet to come for in 1971, the old binding room and folding rooms were demolished and were replaced by a new bay to house ten new printers that could print both sides. Sadly this was the last investment they were to make. Eventually Robert Maxwell became Chief Executive of the British Printing Corporation and in 1981 Clarke and Sherwell closed its doors for the last time.

When Cecil Clarke retired in 1966 the Directorship passed from Peter Harris, David Moor and John Lauden who rose through the ranks until 1980, when he took over.

Of the originators of the firm John S Clarke retired in 1928, William Meredith in 1948, Herbert Smith in 1958, Cecil Clarke in 1966, but George Sherwell remained active in the firm until he died in 1954.

R Z Wills   2011

Dates and info from COLIN EATON
NORTHAMPTON INDEPENDENT 1982

Clarke and Sherwell Factory,
Kingsthorpe Road

From an advert in a Northampton Trade Directory

' We plan, design and produce any kind of printing from an invoice to a bound book. Our wide experience and up-to-date plant enables us to offer excellent service, coupled with sound quality of work at competitive prices. Small orders receive the same care and attention that is given to large contracts like the Jubilee Book, which we recently printed in photogravure for a national newspaper house (for which over 250 tons of paper were required and 7½ tons of ink.) '

Chapter 12

ARTHUR MULLINER

In 1907 Arthur Mulliner one of the founder members of the Royal Automobile Club began making car body parts at his premises in Bridge Street. Before this time for 6 generations the Mulliners had been coach and carriage makers.

Mulliners became known for their quality work and concentrated on maintaining and servicing the better class of car and built up a local and national reputation.

My uncle Cyril worked for Mulliners after his demob from the Army in the 1940s and became a foreman paint sprayer.

He could name the factory colour name of any car he saw on the road and could mix any colour you wanted.

I remember in the 1980s when we were painting our house and ran out of paint Cyril bought 3 tins of paint from the DIY shop and mixed the exact colour match by hand.

When he was coming up to his retirement in the 1970s he was offered jobs by a couple of other garage owners due to his reputation for quality work and he then worked for a few more years at Mr Gibbs garage in Ruskin Road.

Linda Kemp 2011

Chapter 13

ARE YOU BEING SERVED?

April 1958 I was fifteen and had, for the time being, set aside my ambition to become a nurse.

I then accepted employment in the Co-op department store in Abington Street, working in the Drapery Dept.

Growing up in the post-war mean years of ration books, clothing coupons and making do, the big store and arcade shops was where you could get everything money could buy. I was now part of this exciting period in retail. I wore a smart black outfit and was given a basic training in customer-friendly service. Then advised to remember THE CUSTOMER IS ALWAYS RIGHT.

My first position was on Haberdashery, selling a vast selection of buttons, ribbons and cottons to local dressmakers, (Where are they now?) All items purchased would be written down on a bill and mentally added up. The customer's dividend number plus cash was put into the overhead cash tube system and sent by suction to the cash office. The change and receipt would then be sent back to the appropriate counter. This ingenious system worked well most of the time, but impatient customers would sometimes become irate and we would give a rat-a-tat-tat on the tube to speed things up. This was often followed by the office manager, to give us junior staff a sharp telling off! Christmas-time the tubes could not take the volume of cash and a high desk was positioned on each counter and seasonal staff brought in to cope with the rush. I was eventually promoted to Junior Miss alongside Millinery, Lingerie and Ladies Mantles!

I often smile when shopping in H & M, which is situated in the old store, with its bright décor, trendy staff and LOUD music. Things in those days were so different. I was trained to fit school uniforms, bought to last at least two years, hems up and then let down. Children sulking and Mum having the last word.

This, indeed, was a wonderful place to work, six days a week, half-day on Thursdays. We had a good social life and us Young Things were never too tired to strut our stuff of an evening up and down the "Bunny Run" in our hoop skirts, stiff net petticoats and stiletto heels.

WHAT JOY WHEN 'ALL THE WORLD WAS YOUNG'.

Abington Street 1922   *Northampton Co-op far left*

Rosalyn Willis. 2011

Chapter 14

BAXTERS BUTCHERS

The firm started life as London Central Meat Co until the late 1960's when it became Baxters after the name of the chairman. As demand got greater they decided to purchase land at Wootton and they built an abattoir and processing plant which would bring work for hundreds of workers.

The premises in Kings Heath were shut and moved to Wootton.

Life was getting harder in the early 1970's what with strikes and power cuts, the price of food was rising due to the changing over to decimalization. This new plant would bring much needed work for the villagers on the outskirts of the Town. It was to provide a lot of women with work as most families were struggling with just one wage going into the household. This was the time when most women found the need to work. We take this as normal in today's world. It also became the start of children being left on their own while their Mothers worked these were known as Latch key kids.

I had a very young family, my husband had been finished due to Watney Mann closing its brewery in the Town, so he was employed as a Lorry driver at Baxter's during the day. I managed to acquire a job in the evenings becoming an industrial cleaner.

My work was to clean the abattoir along with my friend, it had to be immaculate if it wasn't we had to do it again until it reached the standard required by the Health workers who were employed there.

We had to wear overalls, wellington boots which our trousers were tucked into, also a big heavy rubber apron which came down to our ankles then we had gloves that came up to our elbows.

We did look a sight but was thankful for it as it kept us dry.

When Brooke Bond/Liebeg took over in 1974 we were taken from the abattoir as they didn't think this was a woman's job we were so sad as we had done a good job keeping it spotless . We were given a job in the processing plant and put in the pie room. We had to join their existing cleaners which didn't really work as they resented us joining them. We did this for a few weeks.

Whilst working where flour had been used I found it was drying my hair out even though we were wearing thick nets on our hair. This was making people laugh as my hair was big and being ginger I was nicknamed Dougal (This character was a dog with big ginger hair in the Magic Roundabout a programme from television which was very popular) My friend was called Zebedee who was also from the same programme a man with a spring for legs. These nicknames were to stick until we finally left the firm.

Brooke Bond/Liebeg decided to change the cleaning and put it out for contract. Fortunately we were the only two women that the contract firm employed. They had men to do nearly all the jobs and we were given the sausage machines and the giant beef burger machine to clean every night.

We were back to wearing the big rubber aprons and gloves again but we didn't mind as we were in employment.

We had many a laugh and a few scary moments especially when a cow or bull escaped and ran up the corridors which didn't happen very often, thankfully.

I left employment in Sept 1977 and moved to the Town.

In 1984 Unilever took over and Dewhurst took over in 1985.

My children all worked for Baxters when they were old enough and stayed all but one of them to the end when they were finally made redundant. This happened after British Beef took over and Sainsbury's finally took over, they didn't need the plant at Wootton and 400 odd shops. This became the end of an era, butchers shops were going to become a thing of the past.

The plant was eventually pulled down and the land sold for housing. This is now known as Wootton Fields.

June Wilkes 2011

Chapter 15

THE UNITED COUNTIES OMNIBUS CO

The United Counties Omnibus Co has been operating in Northamptonshire since 1913 when they became the major shareholder in the Wellingborough Omnibus Co.

In 1914 United Counties went out of business and sold its shares in the Wellingborough Bus Co. The Wellingborough Company ran buses during the war but with a reduced service and some of their buses were requisitioned for war work. In 1921 they were taken over by a re-formed United Counties and became the predominant operator in Northants and Beds.

Derngate Bus Station

In 1948 United Counties was sold to the Government and came under State control. In 1952 the Midland area of the Eastern National Omnibus Co. was transferred to United Counties and they now covered Northants, Beds, Hunts and parts of Herts and Bucks.

In 1986 the Company was de-regularised and services run on a commercial basis and out to tender. Also in 1986 the Company was split into three separate entities:-

1. United Counties which covered Northants, Beds and Huntingdon.
2. Milton Keynes City Bus.
3. Luton and District which also covered Hitchen and Aylesbury.
The last major change was in 1987 when the Company was taken over by Stagecoach Holdings of Perth.

Now where shall I go today?

Until the mid-1970s the Company operated from the Bus Station in Derngate which was erected in 1934/5. Buses ran from here to almost every village in the County plus long distance coaches and day and half-day tours.

The Station was very busy but dark and gloomy and the interior was filled by a slight fog of fumes.

The café was a very popular meeting place and was always full of country ladies waiting for the village buses to take them home. Wednesday and Saturday market days were the busiest. The café was a very popular meeting place and was always full of country ladies waiting for the village buses to take them home. Wednesday and Saturday market days were the busiest.

I have a friend whose father and brother both worked as drivers and between them they worked from the 1940s to the late 1990s. My friend's dad often volunteered to drive the tour buses at the weekends as he looked forward to the collection at the end of the day when someone would go round with a flat cap collecting sixpences and the occasional shilling for the driver and sometimes he would end up with as much as thirty shillings.

I worked for the Company for a while in the 1990s in the office at the Bus Station, answering queries about routes, times, fares etc and also complaints and lost property.

The strangest lost property item I ever had was a schoolboy who after a music lesson left a cello on the bus. I have never been able to understand how he could get home before realising he had not got it with him

Linda Kemp 2011

Inside Derngate bus station

Chapter 16

NORTHAMPTON RACE COURSE

Horseracing in Northampton was officially recognised in 1632 and was held at Easter on Harlestone Heath (now known as Harlestone Firs). Each year Northampton Borough Corporation gave a silver gilt cup known as the Harlestone Plate. The value of the cup was £16.13s.4p. Starting in 1672 there were two meetings a year, the second one at Michaelmas.

The "going" appears to have been very rough with many horses and riders coming to grief. This caused a lot of problems and disagreements and following a legal dispute in 1734 racing at Harlestone Heath ceased. Until a few years' ago this circular course was still being used as a gallop.

At the same time as the races at Harlestone Heath, unofficial meetings were taking place over the 118 acres of Common Fields (now known as The Racecourse). In 1658 it came under the rules of the Jockey Club and the races became a popular attraction to people from all walks of life. Its appeal waned towards the end of the 18th Century but was revived again in 1727 when two of the principal races were the Althorp Park Stakes and the Spencer Plate. The latter was given by the then Lord Spencer.

The heyday of the Racecourse was in the last half of the 19th Century. Earl Spencer took his guests such as Edward VII and Baron de Rothschild to the meetings where they would view the races from the Racecourse Pavilion.

In the 1800s the town's Freemen sold the land to the Town Council. Part of the agreement was that the Freemen and their descendants would receive an annuity of £80 a year (to be shared among them). Are there people today receiving a share of this annuity?

In 1882 the Borough Corporation was still supporting the racing by giving a subsidy of £30 to a race called the Corporation Purse. This was held on the last day of the Michaelmas meeting.

As well as attracting prominent members of society the race meetings also attracted a criminal element of tricksters and pickpockets. Also crowd violence was often reported during race days.

The course was not enclosed. It crossed several footpaths and some places had only wooden "dolls" to mark the perimeter. This made it very dangerous and was the cause of several serious accidents. In 1901 a man ran across the course to rescue a child who had wandered on it. The child was unharmed but the man was knocked down and died two days later. The jockey had a broken thigh and broken ribs but was lucky to survive the accident.

The last meeting on the course was on 21 March 1904 when another serious accident occurred. A horse collided with one of the marker "dolls", landed on a spectator and then ran off into the crowd, injuring several people. This was probably the final nail in the coffin. Later that year the Jockey Club ruled the Racecourse was unsuitable for racing and no more meetings would take place there.

Since 1904 the Racecourse has had a variety of uses. During World War I it was taken over by the military. The local people had mixed feelings about this. In 1915 the Welsh Division and their horses were in temporary occupation there. This coincided with an outbreak of throat and lung infections among the local populous. The people claimed the illness was caused by the mess and disease left behind by these troops and it became known as The Racecourse Throat. There was some justification for complaining because the mess they left took some time to clear up and return the area to its original state.

Except for a period during WW1 (from 5 March 1917) when the part of the Course was used as allotments it remained as a public park until the outbreak of WW2. Various sporting activities took place there and it was a popular place for people to go for walks, particularly on Sunday afternoons. Children spent many happy hours at the children's playground that was situated in a large hollow in the centre of the Course. It was known then and is still remembered today as "Happy Valley".

In 1939-45 the Army commandeered 70 acres of the Course and built a barracks and laid tarmac to make parade grounds. This appears to be the only time in its history that any area of the Racecourse has been enclosed. At the end of WW2 there was still another battle to be fought by the Town Council and Reginald Paget, the local Labour MP at that time. The Army wished to continue using the Barracks on the Racecourse but after two years of talks and negotiations, the Government ordered the military to decamp.

Today, the Racecourse remains the large open space it was meant to be and it is still used as a venue for various sports and events. The most popular event was the annual Balloon Festival where over 100 hot air balloons could be seen, attracting thousands of visitors to the town. One of the attractions on offer was a ride in a balloon. This provided an ideal opportunity for a birds' eye-view of the historic and attractive buildings and places that exist within the town and the borders of Northamptonshire. However, this event now takes place on the outskirts of the town at Billing Aquadrome.

P Potter 2010

The Pavilion

WORSHIP

As well as schooldays and work,
all through our lives most of us have had some
connection with church and religion.

The next 8 Chapters touch on these subjects.

Chapter 17

BAPTISTS AND THE BAPTIST CHURCH, KINGSTHORPE

The Baptist Church in the High Street was built in 1835 but Baptists had been meeting in the village since at least 1689 when Meeting Houses for Dissenters were licensed. Most of the Ministers came from Northampton to preach in the village. The Church building was extended over the years with a Sunday School built on the side in 1881. There was a further extension and a porch added in 1892 and more rooms with an upstairs in 1909. The final extension is at the back of the Church facing on to Waitrose.

The wall of the Church in Barnet's Stile has inset stones naming Deacons, Sunday School Teachers etc from when the extension was built and many of the names mentioned are still well-known in Kingsthorpe and Northampton including Chown, Perkins and Britton.

The Baptists were also influential in the Free School which was founded in 1693. One of the long-serving Masters was the Minister of the Church, Rev Joseph Lichfield, who was in charge of the School from 1852 to 1888. The last school built on the site still stands on the corner of The Rise and has been converted into a dwelling name "High Point". I can remember my Grandmother still calling it the School House.

My memories of the Church began with changing into my Sunday best clothes while my Grandmother listened to The Billy Cotton Bandshow and then walking to the Church.

Sometimes after Sunday School my friend Margaret and I used to visit her Great Aunt Gwen in the village for homemade lemonade.

Later I joined the G.L.B. (Girls' Life Brigade) at the Church but this did not last long as I found it too restrictive and also other pastimes had come to be more important at that age such as cinema, music and meeting my friends.

So my connections with the Church came to an end.

Kingsthorpe Baptist Church 2011

Linda Kemp 2010

Chapter 18

ST. PAUL'S CHURCH

This story was told to me by my father, Walter Spittles, it concerns a brass band. My father played the cornet in the 'Northampton Imperial Brass Band'. The brass band in my story was before my time but my father told me that in his day, an age when most churches had a brass band, this was the case with St Paul's Church.

This story is of a tragedy and a lost tradition.

The church rooms had a fire in which all the band instruments were destroyed and it seemed to be unlikely they could be replaced. The publican of the 'Queen Victoria Tavern' on the corner of Kingsthorpe Main Road and Semilong Road was not a religious man by any means, but as the town in those days was made of districts (who looked after themselves) he decided to pay for a new complete set of instruments for the church.

In recognition of such a fine offer the vicar decided that on Sunday mornings the band would form-up and play on the march from the 'Queen Vic,' up to the church as a show of gratitude.

Now comes the loss of tradition!!!

Time passed, the vicar was replaced and after a while the new vicar decided it was not a good thing that a holy brass band should start from a public house and so the tradition was lost.

Reg Spittles 2008

St. Paul's Church from a painting by Paul Souter

Chapter 19

THE BUILDING OF CHRISTCHURCH

I was born in 1918. Although I enjoyed reading I always had more satisfaction in listening to older people of previous years, which in the future would only come from reading books, not always the truth, just someone's opinion.

This is a story told to me in my schooldays by my uncle, Albert Randall. He was a surveyor who worked with the architect, Matthew Holding, who designed the church known as 'Christchurch'. It stands in a very prominent position at the junction of the Wellingborough Road and Christchurch Road.

In the days that it was built, Northampton was a small market town but slowly expanding. The custom was that local businessmen for whatever reason would sponsor something or other, this was the case with 'Christchurch', some of the money would come from sponsors.

My Uncle Albert came from Sheffield, he always referred to money as 'brass'. When they were about to start building, he thought they'd be a bit short of 'brass' and while they had it they should build the front first, unfortunately they didn't.

After a time it appeared a further round of donations would be required and unfortunately one of the sponsors rather than make a donation withdrew. That made certain that 'Christchurch' would not be completed.

Uncle Albert's idea was that if they started at the front and had then run out of 'brass', the rear could have been tidied up with a real chance at a later date to continue further building but they would still have had a complete church.

Reg Spittles 2009

The original Matthew Holding design

When the money ran out.

Chapter 20

SAINT PETER'S CHURCH.

I remember when I was very young, perhaps 7 or 8 my mother and I used to visit Aunt Peg and Uncle Ken in Byfield Road in St James, near the River. They both were involved with St. Peter's church; I think Ken was a sidesman or something. Aunt Peg, a couple of other women, and on occasions my mum and me would go along to the church and polish the pews, sweep and arrange the flowers on a Saturday afternoon for the service on Sunday. My job, which I loved, was to get out the cloths and the tin of Brasso and polish the big brass eagle lectern. I did this in stages as it would have taken ages to polish the whole thing in one go.

The eagle lectern is still there, but I noticed recently that it had been varnished. Now in my later years I see the wonderful carvings in this church with adult eyes, but they still fascinate me, more so now as I am able to appreciate their antiquity and the skill that was needed to carve them. Although St. Sep's is probably older and bigger I feel this church is a more beautiful and interesting structure.

Excavations nearby between 1980 and '82 revealed Anglo-Saxon remains that indicated that there was a church in this area from a much earlier period, probably about 800. It seems probable that this St. Peter's was originally built by Simon de Senlis II, second Norman Earl of Northampton, sometime after 1110. The church's close proximity to the Castle and the large processional arch of a west door that can be seen over the west window indicate that this church may once have functioned as the chapel to the castle, the west door being large enough to admit a Royal procession for worship. This arch would have originally been recessed arch by arch, but was rebuilt flat over the west window, along with the rest of the tower in the late 17th century.

Inside standing before the vestry in the south aisle is a large Saxon stone slab reputed to be the reliquary lid of St. Ragener, nephew of St. Edmund of East Anglia and killed by the Danes in 870. It is believed that this stone was in the church as part of a shrine to St. Ragener until the Reformation when they threw it out. It was rediscovered built into the wall of a nearby brewery when it closed down. The carving is most interesting and fascinated me when I was a kid with its interlaced vines, animals and plants along with a human face – the face of G-D, the Foliate God, The Green Man!

St. Peter's Church 2011

Jack Plowman 2010

Chapter 21

Marian Chapman - Northampton Geography of County and History of Town

St Sepulchre's Church, visited 6th June 1919 by Marian Chapman

"Standard 7 visited St Sepulchres Church on June 6th. The Rev Keysell showed us the church. He told us the church was built by Simon de Senlis as a thank offering because he got home safely from The Crusades. He built it like the Church of the Holy Sepulchre in Jerusalem, which is built on the site of the place where Jesus was buried. The church of that name in Northampton is built on the site of the old Saxon church. The only remains of that is the sun-dial in the porch. There are only four (more) round churches in all England. Simon de Senlis only built the round part and one aisle. More recently two more altars were built. One was dedicated to Thomas a Becket and the other to St John the Baptist.

The Saxons built perpendicular windows, and the arches are round or pointed. In one arch one could see the round part made to a point. On one stained glass window was a picture of King Richard I; in two others close to it were pictures of Richard fighting and underneath were the words "King Richard I at the Battle of Java".

In the round part of the church are chairs, but in the other part are pews. Inside the church was a brass erected to the memory of Mr Coles, his two wives and twelve children. Mr Coles left a sum of money that is given every year on the first Thursday in February to everyone that takes any part in the service.

The church is sometimes called the Soldiers Church because a soldier built it and soldiers go there. There are brass plates on the walls with soldiers names on them who have been killed in the war. There are different flags hanging above. A little niche in the wall was used for the knights to put their staves in when they went to worship there.

The font had a lid hanging from the ceiling that could be lowered at any time. The monks from St Andrew's Priory used to worship at the church. Another object of interest was an old chest the church valuables were kept in.

The vicar also drew our attention to the thick walls and massive pillars."

Church of the Holy Sepulchre at the beginning of 20th century photograph by Henry Cooper

Chapter 22

THE BUILDING OF ST. JOHN THE BAPTIST CHURCH – KINGSTHORPE VILLAGE

The first church on the site was of Saxon origin and was probably a missionary church attached to St. Andrew's Priory and is thought to have consisted of a nave and a chancel. The remains of the windows of this church can still be seen in the nave of the present structure.

It was during the 12th century that the church was extended to incorporate two chapels, on either side of the chancel, which were dedicated to St. Katherine and the Virgin Mary. Later in that century the North and South aisles were constructed to link to the nave and a porch was added.

In the later 14th century the sanctuary was extended to the East end and a crypt constructed under the extension. The crypt survives in an excellent condition and apparently can only be entered from the churchyard.

Within two to three decades the final major rebuilding was accomplished with the addition of a tower and steeple.

The fabric of the church was then virtually unchanged until restoration work was carried out during the Victorian era, most of which was internal and funded by donations from many local benefactors.

In the 19th and 20th centuries many modernisations have taken place culminating in the completion of the church annexe in 1985.

Linda Kemp 2011.

St. John the Baptist Church Kingsthorpe Village

Chapter 23

TOWCESTER ROAD CEMETERY

As you walk up the long drive of Towcester Road Cemetery to the left of the Church is a Memorial dedicated to service people. It is here that you will find nine ANZAC headstones. They commemorate members of the Australian and New Zealand Army Corps who died in this country, whilst not on the battlefield they still lost their lives far from home.

Every year these servicemen are remembered here on the Sunday nearest to Anzac Day which is the 25th April. The service is organized by the Northampton branch of the Western Front Association and is well supported by the Northampton branch of the Royal British Legion. The names are read out and a small wooden

cross is placed beside each headstone, those attending usually wear a sprig of Rosemary for remembrance. At the memorial Poppy wreaths are laid to honour the fallen.
Those remembered are:-

Cpl.William Campbell 5th Australian Engineers, died 11th November 1918
Of Western Australia.

L/Cpl. Samuel Cooke 41st Bn Australian Infantry, died 4th November 1918
From Canada.

Pte. Lyle Cox 58th Bn.Australian Infantry, died 16th November 1918
Of Barnedown Victoria

Pte.Walter Cox 24th Bn Australian Infantry, died 22nd September 1916
Of Gippsland Victoria

Pte. Roy Doust 54th Bn. Australian Infantry, died 30th October 1916
From Clarence River, New South Wales

Cpl. George Easton Australian Machine Gun Corps, died 4th November 1918
Of Camperdown Sydney N.S.W.

Pte. Charles McGoldrick 1st Bn. Australian Infantry, died 16th September 1916
Of Port Kembla N.S.W.

Pte. John Maxwell 26th Bn. Australian Infantry, died 10th September 1916

Pte. Reginald Scanes 53rd Bn. Australian Infantry, died 6th May 1918 Of Erskineville N.S.W.

There is, later in the year in June, another remembrance service to all those who died whilst 'in uniform' since the end of WW2 and who hailed from the county of Northamptonshire. Again this is held in the same place and is organized by the Royal British Legion. Two of the members, Guy Voice and Kevin Lamberth, have painstakingly researched newspapers to find the names of 200 (at the last count) and record them in a book of their making. Relatives are contacted and invited to attend and all the names are read out. Poppy wreaths are laid again at the memorial.

WE WILL REMEMBER THEM.

J.M.Clements. 2011.

Anzac Soldiers' Graves
Towcester Road Cemetery 2011

Chapter 24

FROM KING STREET TO ABINGTON AVENUE

In 1777 a chapel was built in the then King's Head Lane later to be known as King Street. The chapel was enlarged in 1858 and it was reconstructed in 1881. Large and commodious school buildings were erected on the other side of the street in 1863.

Hereby lays a tale of dissention, charges, counter charges, comings, goings, removals, settlements and rebuilding.

The story began way back in 1774 when the then minister of Castle Hill Chapel, Rev. William Hexal a native of Boughton near Kettering, due to failing health was provided with an assistant minister. The Rev. Hexal's troubles seem to stem from this point. Many charges and counter charges were exchanged which led to the majority of the church deacons passing a vote of dismissal against Mr. Hexal. But a large and influential majority of the congregation including church members spurned Rev. Hexal and decided to build another place of worship near by in which the congregation as a whole rather than a small part of it should have the power to appoint or dismiss the minister.

Some of the financing for the new building in King's Head Lane included Mary Doddridge, daughter of Dr. Doddridge, while Lord Spencer, Sir John Robinson, Knightly, Powis, and Isted Esquires showed a considerable support for the new movement.

Mr. Hexal's first service in the new chapel in 1771 was sadly to be his last as he died on the 6th November 1771 aged 67.

The Rev. Thomas Porter succeeded Mr.Hexal and in 1778 he established a register of baptism. He died 14th February 1785.

Between 1785 and 1894 when the Rev Charles S. Larkman was unanimously elected to be minister on 18th February 1894 and commenced his ministry on April 1st there were seven different ministers.

The Rev.William Hexal

Rev. Benjamin Lloyd Edwards   45 years

Rev. John Woodwork   3 years

Rev. Thomas Milner M.A.   10 Years

Rev. George Nicholson B.A.	18 years
Rev. Edward Hill	2 years
Rev. Arthur Vaughn	5 years
Rev. George Nicholson (again)	13 years
Rev. Eustace W. Brennen	5 years

Although during the Rev Nicholson's first ministry at King Street the chapel enlarged at a cost of over £1,000 it still did not meet the needs of the congregation and with little support from the most select and influential in the town Mr. Nicholson resigned. When in 1875 Mr. Nicholson returned for a second time a some of money was raised and in six years the chapel undertook a complete restructure at a cost of £2,000.

By the end of the 19th century the population of Northampton was moving from the centre of the town to the new suburbs, as a result many of the old places of worship were poorly attended but the new neighbourhoods were inadequately provided for.

Recognising this, a piece of land on a main thoroughfare in Abington was secured at a cost of £1,000. A spacious building was to be erected on th left side of the land at a cost of £3,500 (total £4,500). It would be a two story building with a large hall on the upper floor (about the same size as the chapel they were leaving) and would be used for worship until a new chapel, in the future, could be built. The lower floor would be used for Sunday school and similar purposes. An appeal for money to fund this project was put to the congregation and fellow Nonconformists and friends for assistance in this new undertaking. £1,000 had been realised by the sale of the King Street chapel. Other contributors and promises were made by the following friends:-

The Worshipful, the Mayor F.G. Adnitt Esquire J.P.	£100
Mr. F Brickword	£50
" W. H. Bunting	£10
" A. Church	£200
" W. D. Crick	£100
" E. Fitness	£10
" H. H. Goddard	£100
" C. Jones	£100
Rev. C. S. Larkman	£10
Mr. G.N. Souster	£10
" A. Stanton	£100
" M. Wooding	£25
Congregational Church Extension Fund	£200

During the next 10 years money was raised and on Wednesday 21st September 1910 at 3-30pm a service was held for the laying of the foundation stone for the new chapel and a year later on Thursday 21st September 1911 a 'Service of Dedication' was held in the new Abington Avenue Congregational Church.

The Original Design 1900

Although a design for the school rooms and chapel had been produced in 1900, by Chas. Dorman & Son Architects of Northampton, the design for the chapel was not used but a new design by, Messrs. Sutton & Gregory

The 1911 Design

According to the Northampton Independent September 23rd 1911:-

'The strangest part about Northampton's newest Chapel, which opened in Abington Avenue on Thursday, is it looks like a Church'----and --- 'Whether we have progressed in spirit of Christian brotherhood is not clear, for when the original Chapel was opened in King Street over 100 years ago the chapel records give the amazing information that the bells of the neighbouring church of St. Peter where rung in honour of the occasion. Certainly the bells of St. Matthews', which is in the next street to the chapel, also rang on Thursday, waking sleepers in the parish at the hour of six, but it was not to welcome the opening of the new chapel, but to celebrate the 17th anniversary of the dedication of the neighbouring church'.

The chapel/church cost £4,000, £3,000 to be borrowed from the bank and £1,000 to be raised by subscription.

When in 1914 World War 1 was declared the school rooms were commissioned by the government for use as a military hospital. Many of the young men of Abington Avenue Congregational Church left for war service. Many did not return.

After the war Rev. Larkman and the deacons decided to honour those of the congregation who had fallen during 1914-1918. A stained glass window would be installed. A committee was formed by relatives of those who had been killed. Sir Frank Brangwyn was chosen to design the window. It was installed in the end wall of the chancel in 1921 at a cost of £600.

Sir Frank Brangwyn was a friend of Mr. Frederick Fitness, tailor of The Drapery Northampton. Mr. Fitness was the tailor to Brangwyn and also a part time antique dealer who found items for Brangwyn's house, the Jointure, in Sussex. Harold Fitness, son of Frederick Fitness lost his life at Passchendale during the war.

The window is 24 feet high and 10 feet wide with four main lights. The design was reproduced by Messrs. P. Turpin & Co of Berners Street, W.C. The head of firm was Paul Turpin, who carried out many important decorative schemes under Brangwyns' supervision.

Memorial window Abington Avenue U.R.C.

The Rev. Charles S. Larkman

The Rev. Larkman retired on May 16th 1926 and died in Northampton General Hospital in 1936.

In the early part of 20th century Abington Avenue church rooms became the home of Castle Hall School until it closed in 1944.

In 1939 Rev. Owen Butler took up the ministry of Abington Avenue. During his first service it fell to him to announce that war had been declared with Germany. For the second time in just over 20 years the church rooms were requisitioned for war work and young men of the church, again, lost their lives for their country. On Remembrance Sunday in November 1947 a Memorial Plaque was placed in the church, and dedicated, at a special service to honour those who fell in 1939-1945.

The Act of Union took place nationwide in 1972 with the joining together of the Presbyterian and Congregational churches to form the new United Reformed Church. At first Abington Avenue voted against the motion but after much thought and prayer and feed back from the May assembly the church voted overwhelmingly in favour, so Abington Avenue U.R.C. was born.

Another milestone in the history of Abington Avenue began with arrival of Rev. Peter Flint, together with his young family, in May 1987.

In just six months Peter Flint instigated a major rebuilding project of the school/church rooms. Several designs were displayed in church over several weeks. A vote was taken and a design was chosen. It would cost approximately £500,000. A 'Development Gift Day in December 1988 realized £80,000 but was not enough to get the project underway. The design was scrapped.

After much prayer and soul searching the congregation decided to go with an 'in house design' with the help of professional contractors for specific tasks and most of the work D.I.Y.

By the Autumn of 1991 the first phase of the project was complete. It would take 5 years to complete the whole project and in 1995 a thanksgiving service was held in the church. The cost amounted to £650,000 including splendid glass doors installed under the Brangwyn window leading to a central meeting area.

October 1995 saw the arrival of Rev. Mark Westerman and on February 4th 2001 he lead about 80 of the congregation on a walk from the then Moat House Hotel which stands on the site of King Street Chapel. The walk of about three miles to Abington Avenue was to celebrate the move 100 years before.

The very early part of the 20th century saw more changes at A.A.U.R.C. The Sanctuary had a refit. The pews and choir stalls were removed and replaced with chairs and tiered seating, creating another room underneath. A Baptistery was installed, for full immersion baptism, and a new, smaller organ. With the removal of the old organ pipes a new vestry was created. Services can now be held 'in the round ' and the church is very popular for concerts.

The interior before the refit

The interior as it is today

Now as I write this story in 2011, during the ministry of Rev. Dr. Alan Spence the centenary of the Chapel/Church will be celebrated in September 2011.

Abington Avenue United Reformed Church 2011

My thanks to Abington Avenue U.R.C. archives, the congregation and the descendents of King Street and Abington Avenue.

Val Knowles 2011

105

Acknowledgements

Abington Avenue United Reformed Church

Chronicle & Echo

Northampton Libraries & Local Studies Room

Northampton Independent

Front Cover pictures;- Kettering Road School – top

Life on the canal – centre

St. Peter's Church, Northampton - bottom

Other Books By
Northampton Heritage Hunters

A Little Bit of Everything

Published 2009

Castle Ward History Trail

Published 2010

For Book Sales:- 01604 402661